ISKEY O'HARA BONDER

From the desktop of Jeffrey Simmons

A vacation in Paris inspired Miroslav Sasek to create childrens travel guides to the big cities of the world. He brought me *This is Paris* in 1958 when I was publishing in London, and we soon followed up with *This is London*. Both books were enormously successful, and his simple vision grew to include more than a dozen books. Their amusing verse, coupled with bright and charming illustrations, made for a series unlike any other, and garnered Sasek (as we always called him) the international and popular acclaim he deserved.

I was thrilled to learn that *This is Ireland* will once again find its rightful place on bookshelves. Sasek is no longer with us (and I have lost all contact with his family), but I am sure he would be delighted to know that a whole new generation of wide-eyed readers is being introduced to his whimsical, imaginative, and enchanting world.

Your name here

Published by arrangement with Simon & Schuster Books for Young Readers,
Simon & Schuster Children's Publishing Division

This edition first published in 2005 by
UNIVERSE PUBLISHING
A Division of Rizzoli International Publications, Inc.
300 Park Avenue South
New York, NY 10010
www.rizzoliusa.com

*See updated Ireland facts at end of book

2023 2024 2025 / 21 20 19 18

Printed in China

ISBN: 978-0-7893-1224-2

Library of Congress Catalog Control Number: 2004110234

Cover design: centerpointdesign
Universe editor: Jane Newman

M. Sasek

THIS IS
IRELAND

UNIVERSE

IRELAND

Area: 32,500 square miles

Population: 4,000,000

The island is divided into thirty-two counties. Twenty-six form the independent Republic of Eire. The remaining six are part of the United Kingdom.

Counties

1	MAYO	5	CLARE	9	TIPPERARY	13	CARLOW	17	WICKLOW	21	MEATH	25	LEITRIM	29	DOWN
2	SLIGO	6	LIMERICK	10	WATERFORD	14	LEIX	18	DUBLIN	22	LOUTH	26	FERMANAGH	30	ANTRIM
3	ROSCOMMON	7	KERRY	11	KILKENNY	15	OFFALY	19	WESTMEATH	23	CAVAN	27	TYRONE	31	DERRY
4	GALWAY	8	CORK	12	WEXFORD	16	KILDARE	20	LONGFORD	24	MONAGHAN	28	ARMAGH	32	DONEGAL

Since Iron Age times Ireland has been inhabited by Gaels. Roman armies never reached the island, but it was Romanized by Christian missionaries. Before the end of the 6th century, Ireland had become a major seat of Latin learning. Scholars flocked to her great monastic schools, and Irish missionaries brought the Faith and Christian culture to many parts of Europe. This Golden Age was ended at the close of the 8th century by repeated Viking raids. With the Anglo-Norman invasion of 1170 began the centuries-long strife between the English and the Gaels, which later also acquired a fierce religious character. In 1921 Ireland gained Home Rule and the status of a British Dominion through the Anglo-Irish Treaty which established the Irish Free State of 26 counties. The Treaty was followed by a cruel Civil War. It was not till 1949 that Eire officially became a wholly independent Republic.

In Ireland there are fewer people than cattle. The island has been depopulated by two great famines — the first in 1739 killed 400,000 Irishmen; the second, some hundred years later, killed 700,000 — and by emigration. Irishmen began to leave their native shores in great numbers in 1848 on flimsy boats called "floating coffins." In four years, more than 800,000 people left the hunger-struck land.

The country really is green —

Twelve Bens

Connor Pass

every imaginable green —

green and silent.

Even in the towns there is a lot
of green,

TÁ TELEFÓN
AR FÁIL ANSO

YOU MAY TELEPHONE
FROM HERE

but a lot less silence.

St. Patrick, the patron saint of Ireland, landed here in 432, spread Christianity through the island, and of course drove out the snakes.

St. Patrick's Cathedral (founded in 1190) in Dublin, the capital of the Catholic South, is Protestant. It contains the tombs of many illustrious Irishmen. Among them Jonathan Swift, author of "Gulliver's Travels," Dean of the Cathedral in 1713–45.

St. Patrick's Cathedral (founded 700 years later) in Armagh, a city of the Protestant North, is Catholic. Only late in the 19th century did Irish Catholics regain the right to build churches.

Irish saints' names are given to cathedrals and people, places and planes. And there is a wide choice:

St. Fiacre, St. Kevin, St. Finbarr, St. Fintan, St. Doulagh, St. Brendan, St. Columba, St. Canice, St. Enda, St. Maelruain, St. Pappin, St. Moibhi, St. Maigenn, St. Ailbhe...

None of these, not even St. Patrick, has been canonized. All became saints by tradition and popular acclaim. The only formally canonized Irish saint is a 12th-century cleric, St. Lawrence O'Toole.*

AER LINGUS
IRISH INTERNATIONAL AIRLINES
St. Fiacre

In Ireland, not only a harp is "as Irish as a harp";

so are her independent weather,

her "sweet Irish girls,"

and her shop signs.

If there is anything more Irish
than a harp, it's the Little People,
such as this leprechaun;

and if there is anything more Irish
than a leprechaun, it's the shamrock
— the national emblem.

The shamrock appears everywhere.

Legend says St. Patrick used the shamrock to
explain the Holy Trinity.

The Irish shillelagh has often been the last word in arguments,

and Ireland is famous for her fighting men.

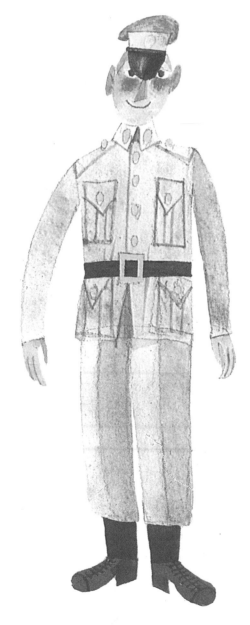

Cobh, the Republic's main port of call for ocean liners.

"Sirius," the first steamer to cross the Atlantic, sailed from Cobh on April 1st, 1838. Her journey took 18½ days.

Eighty-one years later, on June 15th, 1919, the first "aeroplane" to cross the Atlantic landed in Ireland, near Clifden. Its journey from Newfoundland took $16\frac{1}{2}$ hours.

TO LANDING PLACE OF
ALCOCK AND BROWN
FIRST DIRECT
TRANSATLANTIC FLIGHT
(SUNDAY, 15 JUNE, 1919)

Enthusiasts say the Irish invented whiskey.

The oldest distillery of Irish whiskey was founded in
Kilbeggan in 1757.

Irish Coffee — black coffee, sugar, Irish
whiskey, and cream — is only 20 years old.
Place of invention: Shannon Airport.

Europe's biggest brewery is in Dublin.*
Its famous stout is exported to a hundred
countries. Vast beer-cans for a vast trade.

For the 700,000 Dubliners there are 700 pubs in which
to drink their whiskey or stout, or Cork gin for that matter.*

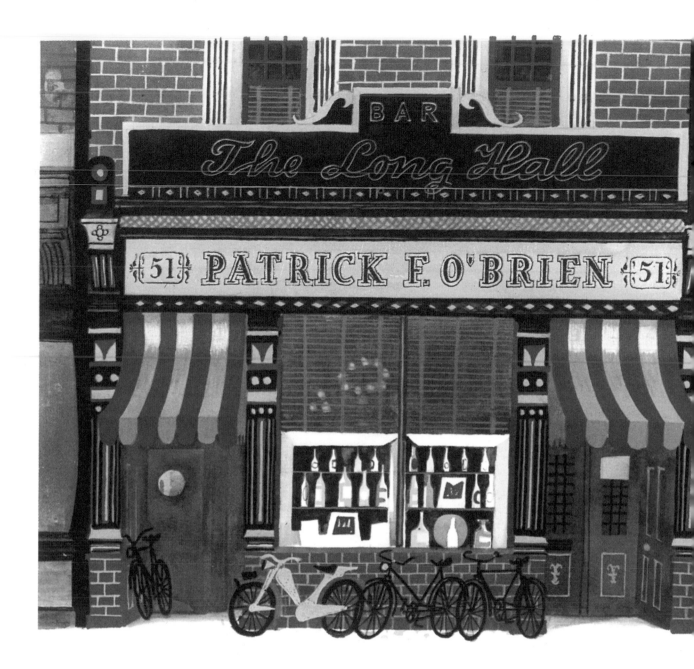

But for the 500,000 Irishmen
who wear

the "Pioneer's Pin" of a teetotaller,

there are only soft drinks in
any pub.

Dublin, Gaelic name *Baile Atha Cliath*, a city of 166 churches, 27 golf clubs, 3 racetracks, and those 700 pubs, began to grow in the 9th century as a base of Viking raiders.* But already in A.D. 140 Ptolemy mentioned a settlement here.

26

Dublin's main thoroughfare, named after a great Irish patriot,
Daniel O'Connell.

His memorial, standing where O'Connell Bridge over the Liffey
becomes O'Connell Street, is the first in a long line of monuments
to great Irishmen. Towering over them all is a British contribution:
the Nelson Pillar, 134 feet high.*

In Dub-lin fair ci-ty where the girls are so pret-ty

A girl from the Moore Street Market

A Dublin flower girl

Men are friendly —

noisy —

public spirited —

nostalgic.

The Record Tower, the only surviving remnant of the 13th-century Dublin Castle. It is joined to the Church of the Most Holy Trinity.

Dublin's most lively period came with the 18th century, when it was the second largest city in the British Isles.

Ely Place

Merrion Square

The Custom House, a masterpiece of the
18th-century architect James Gandon.

The Four Courts, now the seat of Ireland's
High Court of Justice, was completed by the
same architect in 1796.

Both these buildings were heavily damaged during the Civil War of 1921, and later splendidly restored.

The old Parliament House, now the Bank of
Ireland, was the first of a series of great
public edifices erected in Dublin in the 18th century.

This man shows you to a parking
place in front of the Bank.

Trinity College, the University of Dublin, was founded by Elizabeth I. This building dates from the seventeen-fifties. Since 1873 Catholics have been admitted to study here.

Trinity College Library has a vast collection of books and

manuscripts, ancient and modern.

You can also find there the oldest and most elaborately carved Irish harp in existence.

The greatest treasure of the library is the Book of Kells, a copy of the Gospels magnificently illuminated by the monks of the monastery of Kells at the beginning of the 9th century.

Small Ireland has given the great world a multitude of famous sons.

George Bernard Shaw, born at 33 Synge Street, Dublin.

Oscar Wilde, born at 21 Westland Row, Dublin.

Another Dubliner, James Joyce, lived for some time in the
Martello Tower, which now houses the Joyce Museum.

Under Benbulben, in the churchyard of Drumcliff, is the grave of
Ireland's greatest poet, William Butler Yeats.

The most famous of Ireland's great-
grandsons was a Pulitzer Prize winner
and later 35th President of the United
States. His great-grandfather was born
in this cottage in Dunganstown, near
New Ross, County Wexford.

Clonmacnois is among Ireland's most celebrated holy sites. Its monastery, founded by St. Ciaran in 548, was for centuries one of Europe's great places of Latin and Christian learning. It is the burial place of many old Irish kings.

For students of pre-history there are in Ireland thousands of monuments whose dates range from 3,000 B.C. to Christian times.

The Rock of Cashel was the seat of kings from A.D. 370 to 1101, when it was granted to the Church. Here St. Patrick baptized King Aengus. Here Brian Boru was crowned.

The first of many Norman castles in Ireland, built in 1169, overlooking Ferrycarrig Bridge and the River Slaney.

Lismore Castle, built by King John in 1185, once belonged to Sir Walter Raleigh. From 1753 it became the Irish seat of the Dukes of Devonshire.

Blarney Castle, a 15th-century stronghold, built by Cormac Laidhir MacCarthy, Lord of Muskerry.

Tradition says, "kiss the Blarney Stone and get invincibly eloquent." You may also get lumbago.

Ashford Castle in County Mayo is now a hotel. Guests can fish, shoot, and live here like lords.

At Bunratty Castle in County Clare one can partake of a lordly
15th-century banquet at the table of the Earl of Thomond.

And here is the menu*:

Selections of Mediaeval Dishes

1st. Remove

Braume Brose — Soupes Dorroy
Balloke Broth
Sew Lumbarde — Henny's in Bruette

2nd. Remove

Fylettes of Porke — Pompeys
Herbelade
Doucettes — Tarte Fysche

Allowes
Bake Mete — Blaunde Sorre
Pety-toes in Gelyce

3rd. Remove

Salomene — Beef Ryale
Henny's in Grauncelye
Chekyn's in Browet — Vell Presse
Turbot — Roste Ensauce
☆ ☆ ☆

Joutes — Cabochis — Wortes
❀ ❀ ❀

Salat Salamagundy

4th. Remove

Syllabubs — Rastons — Perls in Syrippe
Quyade — Trayne Roste
☆ ☆ ☆

Manchets

The Giant's Causeway, in County Antrim, is one of the natural wonders of the world. According to legend, it was constructed by the giant Finn MacCoul; according to geologists, by Lava MacCool.

Nearby on a rock, the picturesque ruins
of the 14th-century Dunluce Castle.

Ireland is not only a country of green meadows
and hills, but also a country of lakes.

View of Lough Leane from Ross Castle in Killarney, renowned holiday resort of County Kerry.

A local taxi, a traditional Irish jaunting car.

Pontoon, in County Mayo, takes its name from the bridge between Lough Conn and Lough Cullen.

Irish lakes and rivers are full of salmon, sea trout, brown trout, and coarse fish.

Ireland's coastline, broken up by innumerable inlets, bays, and rivers, is over 2,000 miles long.

Kinsale is well known for its deep-sea fishing. William Penn, the founder of Pennsylvania, was a Clerk of the Admiralty Court here.

One of the loveliest parts of the country is the southwest corner, where the Gulf Stream washes the shore. The climate is mild and the vegetation is subtropical.

Glengarriff at the head of Bantry Bay

A view of Glengarriff Harbour at sunset

The Cliffs of Moher, spectacular and sheer, at places 700 feet high, the nesting-place of a huge variety of sea-birds. This limestone and shale formation stretches five miles along the west coast.

Thirty miles off the coast lie the Aran Islands: Inishmere, Inishmann, and Inisheer, whose Gaelic-speaking fishermen use the currach, the typical Irish boat made of laths and tarred canvas.

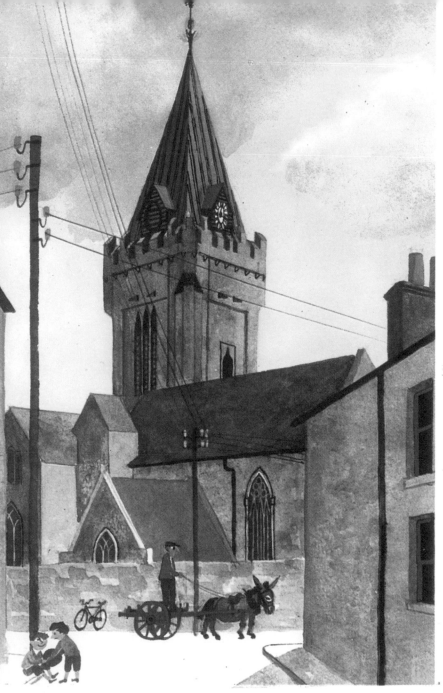

Galway, the main city of the Atlantic coast

The Church of St. Nicholas, founded in 1320, where — it is charmingly said — Christopher Columbus prayed on his way to discover the New World.

A tablet on a wall behind the church commemorates the deed of Mayor James Lynch Fitzstephen who in 1493 condemned his own son to death for murder and, when no other would do it, himself hanged him. Hence the expression "Lynch Law."

Connemara is the name of the
western part of County Galway.

Here more than anywhere else you can see the old way of
"mining" Irish "coal," cutting peat with a spade.

Machine-cut peat serves the power plants.

In fact, Connemara is Ireland's "Far West." Green stillness, stony pastures, lonely thatched cottages inhabited by speakers of Gaelic.

This is the sort of traffic you are likely to meet during "rush hour" on an Irish road —

unless a rainbow decides to end along your road, in which case you will meet one of the Little People, guarding the traditional crock of gold.

Because —

this is Ireland.

THIS IS IRELAND...TODAY!

*Page 15: Other canonized Irish saints are St. Malachy and St. Oliver Plunkett.

*Page 23: Today Europe's biggest brewery is Baltika, in St. Petersburg, Russia, though its biggest stout brewery is in Dublin.

*Page 24: Today there are 1,000,000 Dubliners and 1,000 pubs in Dublin.

*Page 26: Today there are 200 churches, 56 golf clubs, and one racetrack in Dublin.

*Page 27: Today Nelson Pillar no longer stands. It was demolished in an explosion on March 8, 1966.

*Page 45: Today the banquet menu at Bunratty Castle has changed, a lot! The dishes are written in English, and this is what you might be served:

- Glass of Mead
- Spiced Parsnip Soup
- Traditional Spare Ribs with Honey and Whiskey Sauce
- Chicken with Apple and Mead Sauce
- Fruit of the Forrest Mousse
- Red/White Wine

AND

Today double-decker buses (pages 13, 26–27, and 34–35) may be painted red, or yellow with blue shades. Since 1964 their color has changed several times.
Today "Irish International" does not appear on the airplanes of Aer Lingus (pages 15 and 18). It hasn't since 1974.